Role-Play Revision
for GCSE German

Gillian Benbow

CASSELL

First published 1990 by Cassell Publishers Limited
Artillery House, Artillery Row, London SW1P 1RT, England

© Cassell Publishers Limited 1990

British Library Cataloguing in Publication Data
Benbow, Gillian
  Role-play revision for GCSE German.
  1. Spoken German language
  I. Title
  438.3´421

ISBN 0-304-31871-X

Typeset by Litho Link Limited, Welshpool, Powys, Wales.
Printed and bound in Great Britain by Cox & Wyman Ltd,
Reading.

Contents

To the teacher and the pupil   1

Useful phrases   3

Expressing your feelings   4

Public transport   6

At the garage/filling station   10

At the customs   13

At the campsite   14

At the youth hostel   17

At the doctor's/at the scene of an accident   20

Shopping for food and drink   24

Shopping for clothes and toiletries   28

At the cleaner's/launderette   31

At the café/restaurant   32

At the post office   37

On the telephone   39

At the bank/exchange office   41

At the police station/lost property office   43

At the tourist information office   46

Asking the way   48

At the cinema   51

At the hotel   53

Visiting and receiving an exchange partner   57

Die Antworten   63

To the teacher and the pupil

I have selected the role-play situations and prompts in this book using my experience as a teacher of German in a comprehensive school. The material in this book covers the syllabuses of all the UK exam groups.

The role-play part of the oral test requires a lot of practice and it is not always easy to find prompts in English to practise on. It is for this reason that this book has been written. Each unit has been divided into three parts:

- Essential vocabulary.
- A list of English prompts.
- A list of suggested answers to those prompts (at the back of the book).

Needless to say, there is always more than one way of communicating an idea in a foreign language. I have selected the expression that I feel GCSE/Standard candidates will find easiest to remember and to use.

The following abbreviations are used in the vocabulary sections: n.p. = no plural; + acc = followed by the accusative case; + dat = followed by the dative case; + gen = followed by the genitive case; sep = separable verb.

I suggest that the pupil approach each unit as follows. First, learn the vocabulary section. You will find that you will be floundering later on if you don't. Then, look at the English prompts. Don't try to work through a whole section. Take, say, five or ten prompts. See if you can answer them and then look up the answers at the back of the book to see how you fared. The book can be used for pair-work in class and is ideal for homework setting.

In your exam, you may have to express a feeling as well as communicate a fact. For instance, the prompt might say:

'Say that you do not agree and ask to see the manager.'

To cater for this, I have included a special section called 'Expressing your feelings'. In addition, there is a list of useful phrases, which will be valuable in many role-play situations.

Viel Glück!

Gillian Benbow
Wolverley High School, Kidderminster, Worcestershire

Useful phrases

Wo ist . . .?	Where is . . .?
Wie komme ich (zum . . .)? **(zur . . .)?**	How do I get to . . .?
Um wieviel Uhr ist . . .?	What time is . . .?
Wie weit entfernt ist . . .?	How far is . . .?
Wie lange . . .?	How long . . .?
Können Sie . . .?	Can you . . .?
Können Sie mir sagen . . .?	Can you tell me . .
Wollen Sie bitte . . .?	Please will you . . .?
Wollen Sie mir bitte . . . geben?	Please will you give me . . .?
Ich möchte/Ich hätte gern/Ich würde gern . . .	I would like . . .
Ich suche . . .	I am looking for . . .
Können Sir mir helfen?	Can you help me?
Wollen Sie das wiederholen?	Would you repeat that?
Sprechen Sie bitte langsamer.	Please speak more slowly.
Ich verstehe.	I understand.
Ich verstehe nicht.	I don't understand.
Ist gut!	OK!
Gibt es . . .?	Is there . . .?
Ich habe . . . verloren.	I have lost . . .

Expressing your feelings

Paß auf!	Be careful!
Wie schade!	What a pity!
Ich habe lieber . . .	I prefer . . .
Ich habe nicht gern . . .	I don't like . . .
Ich hasse . . .	I hate . . .
Ich habe gern . . .	I like . . .
Ich habe sehr gern . . .	I love . . .
Hoffentlich . . .	I hope that/hopefully
Es hat mir gefallen.	I liked it.
Es hat mir nicht gefallen.	I didn't like it.
Ich bin enttäuscht.	I am disappointed.
Ich bin froh.	I am glad.
Ich habe vergessen.	I forgot.
Entschuldigung!	Sorry!
Es tut mir leid, aber . . .	I am sorry but . . .
Hilfe!	Help!
Einverstanden!	Agreed!
Ich bin einverstanden.	I agree.
Ich bin nicht einverstanden.	I don't agree.
Herzlichen Glückwunsch!	Congratulations!
Zum Wohl!	Your health!
Viel Glück!	Good luck!
Gute Reise!	Have a good trip!
Guten Appetit!	Enjoy your meal!
Was für eine Überraschung!	What a surprise!
Bitte schön!	Don't mention it.
Ich langweile mich.	I'm bored.

Keine Sorge!	Don't worry.
Pech!	Bad luck!
Gute Idee!	Good idea!
Ich nehme an.	I accept.
Ich lehne ab.	I refuse.
Es ist mir egal.	I don't mind.
Ich habe Angst.	I'm afraid.
Viel Spaß!	Have fun!
Quatsch!	Rubbish!
Toll!	Great! Super!

6 Public transport

BUYING TICKETS

first-class ticket	die Fahrkarte(n) erster Klasse
second-class ticket	die Fahrkarte(n) zweiter Klasse
single ticket	die Einzelfahrkarte/ einfach
return ticket	die Rückfahrkarte/ hin und zurück
ticket-office	der Fahrkarten- schalter(-)

FACILITIES

information office	das Verkehrsamt ("er)/ das Auskunftsbüro(s) die Auskunftsstelle(n)
left luggage office	die Gepäckauf- bewahrung(en)
lost property office	das Fundbüro(s)
snack bar	die Imbißstube(n)
timetable	der Fahrplan("e)
waiting-room	der Warteraum("e)/ der Wartesaal (Wartesäle)

TRAVELLING BY RAIL

carriage	der Wagen
compartment	das Abteil(e)
dining-car	der Speisewagen
platform	der Bahnsteig(e)
porter	der Gepäckträger(-)
railway	die Eisenbahn
sleeping-car	der Schlafwagen
track	das Gleis(e)

TRAVELLING BY AIR

air hostess	die Stewardeß (essen)
airport	der Flughafen(")
flight	der Flug("e)

TRAVELLING BY BUS, UNDERGROUND OR TAXI

bus	der Bus (Busse)
bus station	der Busbahnhof("e)
bus stop	die Bushaltestelle(n)
taxi rank	der Taxistand("e)
underground	die U-Bahn
underground station	die U-Bahnstation (en)

TRAVELLING BY SEA

hovercraft	das Luftkissen- fahrzeug(e)
ferry	die Fähre(n)
ship	das Schiff(e)

VERBS

to arrive	ankommen
to book	reservieren
to change (i.e. trains)	umsteigen
to fly	fliegen
it is necessary	es ist nötig/man muß
to land (planes)	landen
to leave	abfahren
to leave (e.g. luggage)	aufgeben

to miss (i.e. a train)	**verpassen**	early	**früh**
to stop	**halten**	entrance	**der Eingang (¨e)**
to take off (i.e. planes)	**abfliegen**	exit	**der Ausgang(¨e)**
to wait	**warten**	Have a good trip!	**gute Reise!**
		late/delayed	**verspätet**
		luggage	**das Gepäck(n.p.)**
OTHER WORDS		passport	**der (Reise) paß (pässe)**
bag	**die Tasche(n)**	seat	**der Platz(¨e)**
by air	**mit dem Flugzeug**	suitcase	**der Koffer(-)**
by train	**mit dem Zug**	taken (i.e. a seat)	**besetzt**
direct	**direkt**	traveller	**der/die Reisende(n)**
door (of a vehicle)	**die Tür(en)**		

Du bist dran

1 Ask for a second-class single to Bonn.

2 Ask for a first-class return to Düsseldorf.

3 Say you want two tickets.

4 Find out if there is a bus/train to München.

5 Find out what time it arrives.

6 Find out when the train departs.

7 Ask how often the trains to Bonn are.

8 Say you would like to reserve a seat.

9 Say that you have a reserved seat.

10 Find out where the station/the bus station/the underground station is.

11 Ask how long the journey takes.

12 Find out when the next flight is.

13 Ask where the ticket-office is.

14 Ask where the information office is.

15 Find out where the left luggage/lost property office is.

16 Find out which platform the Bonn train leaves from.

17 Ask where the taxi rank/bus stop is.

18 Find out if there is a seat free in the carriage.

19 Say that the seat is taken.

20 Find out what time the plane takes off/lands.

21 Say that you would like to take a taxi.

22 Ask where you can find a taxi.

23 Find out if the train is direct.

24 Ask if it is necessary to change.

25 Ask where you must change.

26 Ask the driver to take you to a cheap hotel.

27 Ask for the snack bar.

28 Find out when the next/first/last bus leaves.

29 Say you want a non-smoking compartment.

30 Ask where you can leave your luggage.

31 Ask if this is the right platform.

32 Ask where you should get off.

33 Find out if there is a dining-car/a sleeping car.

34 Ask if there is a reduction/a supplement.

35 Find out where the toilets are.

36 Find out where the waiting-room is.

37 Ask if you can hand in your luggage here.

38 Find out if the flight is late.

39 Ask if the train arrived early.

40 Say that you have lost your ticket.

41 Find out the price of a book of tickets.

42 Ask for a map of the underground.

43 Say you will arrive at 10 p.m.

44 Say you will set off at 2 a.m.

45 Ask your friend if he/she has anything to declare.

46 Say that you have just arrived.

47 Say that you will catch the ten o'clock bus.

48 Tell your friend that you tried to phone from the station.

49 Tell your friend that you will phone from the airport.

Zweimal einfach nach Düsseldorf, bitte.

50 Find out where you can find a porter.

51 Ask the porter to help you with your luggage.

52 Say that you have missed the bus.

53 Find out if the bus goes to the town centre.

Wollen Sie auf Seite 63 verweisen.

At the garage/filling station P. 65

G R U N D W O R T S C H A T Z

B R E A K D O W N

battery	**die Batterie(n)**
breakdown	**die Panne(n)**
brakes	**die Bremsen**
flat tyre	**die Reifenpanne(n)**
headlight	**der Scheinwerfer(-)**
mechanic	**der Mechaniker(-)**
out of petrol	**das Benzin ist ausgegangen**
windscreen	**die Windschutz- scheibe (n)**

R O U T I N E S T O P

oil	**das Öl**
leadfree (petrol)	**Bleifrei**
petrol	**das Benzin**
petrol (four-star)	**Super (das Superbenzin)**
pressure (of tyres)	**der Reifendruck**

road-map	**die Straßenkarte(n)**
toilets	**die Toiletten**
tyre	**der Reifen(-)**
water	**das Wasser(-)**

R O A D S

A-road	**die Bundesstraße(n)**
motorway	**die Autobahn(en)**

V E R B S

to break down	**eine Panne haben**
to check (i.e. the oil)	**nachsehen**
to clean	**putzen**
to fill up (with petrol)	**volltanken**
to park	**parken**
to repair	**reparieren**
to work (i.e. the brakes)	**funktionieren**

Du bist dran

1 Ask for 20 litres of high-grade petrol.

2 Ask for 10 litres of leadfree petrol.

3 Ask the attendant to fill up the tank.

4 Ask the attendant to check the oil.

5 Ask the attendant to check the tyres.

6 Ask the attendant to check the water.

7 Find out where the toilets are.

8 Ask if they sell road-maps.

9 Find out if you are on the right road for Bonn.

10 Ask which way to go to Düsseldorf.

11 Find out if the road to Bonn is an A-road or a motorway.

12 Find out where you can park.

13 Say your car has broken down.

14 Say you have left it two kilometres away.

15 Ask if he can help.

16 Ask if he can fix your car.

17 Ask if there is a mechanic available.

18 Say the brakes don't work.

19 Say you have a puncture.

20 Tell the attendant that a headlight is not working.

21 Say that the windscreen is broken.

22 Say you need a new battery.

23 Find out how much you owe.

24 Ask if you can phone from here.

25 Find out how far it is to Bonn.

26 Find out where the nearest hotel is.

27 Ask if they sell sweets.

28 Ask the attendant to clean the windscreen.

29 Say you have run out of petrol.

30 Say you have had an accident.

31 Ask how long you will have to wait.

32 Ask how much it costs.

Wollen Sie auf Seite 65 verweisen.

Können Sie bitte das Wasser prüfen?

At the customs *P.67*

GRUNDWORTSCHATZ

LUGGAGE		present	das Geschenk(e)
bag	die Tasche(n)	watch	die Armbanduhr(en)
luggage	das Gepäck (n.p)		
suitcase	der Koffer(-)		
		OTHER WORDS	
PROPERTY		customs	der Zoll
passport	der Reisepaß(¨sse)	customs officer	der Zollbeamte(n)
perfume	das Parfüm	to declare	verzollen

Du bist dran

1 Say you are English/Irish/Scottish/Welsh.

2 Say you have nothing to declare.

3 Say you would like to declare a camera.

4 Tell the officer that you have two suitcases and a bag.

5 Say that this suitcase is yours.

6 Tell the officer that there are clothes and presents in your suitcase.

7 Say that you bought the watch in Switzerland a week ago.

8 Tell the officer that the perfume cost four hundred marks.

9 Ask if he/she wants to see your passport.

10 Tell the officer that you will be in Germany for two weeks.

11 Say that you are here on holiday.

Wollen Sie auf Seite 67 verweisen.

14 At the campsite

EQUIPMENT

battery	die Batterie(n)
camping equipment	die Campingausrüstung
caravan	der Wohnwagen(-)
corkscrew	der Korkenzieher(-)
gas bottle	das Campinggas
tent	das Zelt(e)
tin-opener	der Dosenöffner(-)/ der Büchsenöffner(-)

FACILITIES

drinking water	das Trinkwasser
dustbin	die Mülltonne(n)
electric socket	die Steckdose(n)
pitch (for tent)	der Platz(¨e)
toilet	die Toiletten

OTHER WORDS

campsite	der Campingplatz(¨e)

clean	sauber
dirty	schmutzig
extra payment	der Zuschlag(e)
match (for lighting a fire)	das Streichholz(¨er)
shade	der Schatten
washing (i.e. clothes	die Wäsche
well-equipped	gut ausgestattet
well-lit	hell beleuchtet

VERBS

to camp	zelten
to do the washing-up	abspülen (sep)
to need	brauchen
to put up (a tent)	das Zelt aufbauen (sep)/ aufschlagen (sep)
to stay	bleiben

Du bist dran

1 Say you would like to reserve a pitch.

2 Ask if you can camp here.

3 Find out if they have space for a tent.

4 Say you have a tent/caravan.

5 Ask how much it is for a tent, two adults, four children and a car.

6 Say you would like to stay for two days.

7 Say you are alone.

8 Say that you will arrive the day after tomorrow.

9 Tell the warden that you will leave on Saturday.

10 Ask where your pitch is.

11 Say you would like a pitch in the shade.

12 Say you are English/Irish/Scottish/Welsh.

13 Ask if he/she wants to see your identity card/passport.

14 Find out when you must pay.

15 Say you would like to pay now.

16 Ask how you get to the campsite.

Sie haben den Schlüssel für Ihren Wohnwagen verloren? Vielleicht wollen Sie diesen Dosenöffner verwenden.

17 Find out if there are hot showers.

18 Say you want a pitch near the toilets.

19 Find out where you can find drinking water.

20 Ask where you can wash clothes/dishes.

21 Ask about the regulations.

22 Say that your pitch is too near the dustbins.

23 Ask if you can borrow a tin-opener/corkscrew/some matches.

24 Ask if you can put up your tent over there.

25 Find out where the nearest electric socket is.

26 Ask how much it is per person.

27 Say it is too expensive.

28 Ask if there is a washing-machine on the site.

29 Ask if they serve hot meals.

30 Find out if there is a shop on the site.

31 Ask if you can light a fire.

32 Tell the warden that you are very pleased with the campsite.

33 Ask if the campsite has lots of facilities.

34 Say you need a gas bottle.

35 Say you need batteries.

36 Find out if the campsite is well-lit at night.

37 Ask if the campsite is closed at night.

38 Ask if you have to pay extra for that.

Wollen Sie auf Seite 67 verweisen.

At the youth hostel *P-69*

GRUNDWORTSCHATZ

BEDDING

blanket	die (Bett)decke(n)
sheets	die Bettwäsche / Bettlaken (Laken)
sleeping-bag	der Schlafsack(¨e)

PLACES

bathroom	das Badezimmer(-)
dining-room	der Speisesaal (säle)
dormitory	der Schlafraum(¨e)
games room	das Spielzimmer(-)
kitchen	die Küche(n)
shower	die Dusche(n)
toilets	die Toiletten

AT RECEPTION

all year	das ganze Jahr (hindurch)
bed	das Bett(en)
card (membership)	die Mitgliedskarte(n)
closed	geschlossen
form (to fill in)	das Formular(e)
full	voll

open	offen
per day	pro Tag
per night	pro Nacht
per person	pro Person
regulations	die Hausordnung

OTHER WORDS

breakfast	das Frühstück
dustbin	die Mülltonne(n)
hot water	warmes Wasser
meal	die Mahlzeit(en)
valuables	die Wertsachen
youth hostel	die Jugendherberge(n)

VERBS

to book	reservieren
to complain	sich beschweren
to cook	kochen
to have dinner	das Abendessen einnehmen / zu Abend essen
to hire	mieten / leihen
to pay	zahlen
to sleep	schlafen

Du bist dran

1 Say you have reserved a bed.

2 Say you have not reserved a bed.

3 Ask if there is any room.

4 Ask if there are any free beds.

5 Say you will leave tomorrow/the day after tomorrow.

6 Say you will stay for three nights.

7 Tell the warden that there are two boys and two girls in your party.

8 Say you are English/Irish/Scottish/Welsh.

9 Find out how much it is per person per night.

10 Ask if there are shops nearby.

11 Find out if there are showers, a kitchen and a games room in the hostel.

12 Ask where the toilets/the dustbins are.

13 Tell the warden that you would like to pay now/later/tomorrow.

14 Find out what time breakfast/lunch/dinner is served.

Darf ich bitte Bettlaken entleihen?

15 Ask what time the hostel closes.

16 Ask what time the office opens in the morning.

17 Ask what the regulations are.

18 Tell the warden that you have a sleeping-bag.

19 Say that you would like to hire a sleeping-bag/some sheets/some blankets.

20 Ask where the girls' and the boys' dormitories are.

21 Find out if alcohol is allowed.

22 Ask what time you must leave the hostel.

23 Find out if you have to fill in a form.

24 Enquire if there is hot water.

25 Ask what you must do before leaving.

26 Find out where you can leave valuables.

27 Say you have a complaint.

28 Ask the warden if he/she wants to see your identity card.

29 Find out if the hostel is full.

30 Ask if the hostel is open all year.

31 Enquire if you can cook in the hostel.

32 Ask if meals are available.

33 Ask directions to the dining-room.

34 Ask where you can leave your bicycle.

35 Say you are sorry, you do not want to sleep upstairs. Ask for a bed on the ground floor.

Wollen Sie auf Seite 69 verweisen.

R-71

At the doctor's/at the scene of an accident

BUYING MEDICINE

antiseptic	das Antiseptikum
aspirin	die Kopfschmerz-tablette(n)
bandage	der Verband("e)/die Binde(n)
chemist's	die Apotheke(n)
cotton wool	die Watte
cream/ointment (i.e. for sores)	die Salbe(n)
medicine	die Arznei(en)/die Medizin/das Medikament(e)
plaster (for cuts)	das Heftpflaster(-)
prescription	das Rezept(e)
receipt	die Quittung(en)
tablet	die Tablette(n)

COMPLAINTS

flu	die Grippe
having a cold	erkältet sein
injured	verletzt
seasickness	die Seekrankheit
sunburn	der Sonnenbrand
sunstroke	der Sonnenstich
temperature	das Fieber

SCENE OF AN ACCIDENT

ambulance	der Kranken-wagen(-)
collision	der Zusammenstoß
doctor	der Arzt("e)
driving licence	der Führerschein
fault	die Schuld
fire	das Feuer
firemen	die Feuerwehr-männer
insurance	die Versicherung
serious	ernst/schlimm

OTHER WORDS

better	besser
dentist	der Zahnarzt("e)
stomach	der Magen
throat	der Hals("e)
tooth	der Zahn("e)

VERBS

to brake	bremsen
to break	brechen
to burn	brennen
to cough	husten
to cut oneself	sich schneiden
to fall	fallen
to feel	sich fühlen
to hurt oneself	sich verletzen
to knock over	anfahren
to stay in bed	das Bett hüten
to sting (i.e. insects)	stechen
to sting (i.e. nettles)	verbrennen
to vomit	sich übergeben/brechen

Du bist dran

1 Ask if he/she can help you.

2 Ask him/her to phone a doctor.

3 Ask him/her to phone for an ambulance.

4 Say you need a dentist.

5 Say you would like to see the doctor.

6 Say you have had an accident.

7 Say you have a toothache.

8 Say you have a sore throat.

9 Say you have a headache.

10 Say you have a pain in your stomach.

11 Say you have broken your arm/leg.

12 Say he has broken his arm/leg.

13 Say you have a cold.

14 Say you have burnt yourself.

15 Say you have burnt your arm.

16 Say he has sunstroke/sunburn.

17 Say she has flu.

18 Say you have cut yourself.

19 Say you have cut your leg/finger.

20 Say that you fell.

21 Say that you have had a car accident.

22 Say that you have a temperature.

23 Say that you are seasick.

24 Say that you have been stung by an insect.

25 Say that you have a cough.

26 Say that you have been sick three times.

27 Say that your friend is injured.

28 Ask if you must come back to see the doctor again.

29 Find out if you have to stay in bed.

30 Find out if you need a prescription.

31 Find out where the chemist's is.

32 Ask for a receipt.

33 Find out how long you must take the tablets for.

34 Say you would like to buy some cotton wool, a bandage, some plasters and some antiseptic.

35 Say that your sister feels ill.

36 Ask for some aspirin.

37 When asked how long you have been ill, say for two hours/ since yesterday.

38 Ask how often you should take the tablets.

39 Say that you feel ill/better.

40 Find out if he has anything for a sore throat.

41 Say that you are taking no medicines.

42 Say that you have insurance.

43 Ask him/her to phone the police/fire brigade.

44 Say that the accident was serious.

45 Say it was not your fault; say it was the fault of the other driver.

46 Find out if they sell a cream for sunburn.

47 Say that your father braked but there was a collision.

48 Say there was a fire in the engine.

49 Say that your father's driving licence is at the hotel.

50 Say that a cyclist knocked over an old man who was crossing the street.

51 Say that it hurts.

Wollen Sie auf Seite 71 verweisen.

Wollen Sie bitte einen Krankenwagen rufen?

Shopping for food and drink

P. 73

GRUNDWORTSCHATZ

SHOPS

baker's	die Bäckerei(en)
butcher's	die Metzgerei(en)
cake shop	die Konditorei(en)
chemist's	die Apotheke(n) / die Drogerie(n)
department store	das Kaufhaus(¨er)
fishmonger's	das Fischgeschäft(e)
greengrocer's	die Obst- und Gemüsehandlung(en)
grocer's	das Lebensmittelgeschäft(e)
market	der Markt(¨e)
supermarket	der Supermarkt(¨e)
tobacconist's	der Tabakladen

FRUIT

apple	der Apfel(¨e)
apricot	die Aprikose(n)
banana	die Banane(n)
cherry	die Kirsche(n)
fruit	das Obst (n.p.)
grape	die Traube(n)
melon	die Melone(n)
orange	die Apfelsine(n)
peach	der Pfirsich(e)
pear	die Birne(n)

pineapple	die Ananas(-)
strawberry	die Erdbeere(n)

VEGETABLES

bean	die Bohne(n)
cabbage	der Kohl (Kohlköpfe)
carrot	die Karotte(n) (Mohrrübe(n))
cauliflower	der Blumenkohl(-)
lettuce	der grüne Salat(e) / der Kopfsalat(e)
mushroom	der Pilz(e) / (der Champignon(s))
onion	die Zwiebel(n)
pea	die Erbse(n)
potato	der Kartoffel(n)
vegetable	das Gemüse(n.p)

MEAT

beef	das Rindfleisch
chicken	das Hähnchen
ham	der Schinken
lamb	das Lammfleisch
liver	die Leber
meat	das Fleisch
sausage	die Wurst
steak	das Steak(s)
veal cutlet	das Schnitzel(-)

DESSERT		milk	**die Milch**
cake	**der Kuchen(-)**	mineral water	**das Mineralwasser**
cheese	**der Käse**	tea	**der Tee**
	(Käsesorten)	wine	**der Wein**
dessert	**der Nachtisch(e) /**		
	das Dessert(s)	**OTHER WORDS**	
ice-cream	**das Eis**	egg	**das Ei(er)**
		pepper	**der Pfeffer**
DRINK		salt	**das Salz**
beer	**das Bier**	seafood	**die Meeresfrüchte**
coffee	**der Kaffee**	slice	**die Scheibe(n)**
drink	**das Getränk(e)**		
fruit juice	**der Obstsaft(¨e)**		

Du bist dran

1 Say you would like a loaf of bread.

2 Ask how much it is.

3 Say you would like to buy some cakes.

4 Ask for five hundred grammes of ham.

5 Say you would like some beef/mutton/chicken.

6 Ask for two hundred and fifty grammes of sausage.

7 Find out if there is a grocer's shop open in the area.

8 Say you would like to buy some cigarettes for your father.

9 Ask for two hundred grammes of cherries/bananas/
oranges/peaches/pears/apples/strawberries/
apricots/grapes.

10 Ask for a pineapple/a melon.

11 Find out where you can buy vegetables.

12 Ask for a pound of beans/onions/peas/potatoes/
mushrooms/cabbage/carrots/cauliflower.

13 Ask for a lettuce.

14 Find out if there is a butcher's shop nearby.

15 Ask for a kilogramme of chicken/rabbit/steak.

16 Ask if the meat is good in that shop.

17 Find out where you can buy seafood.

18 Ask for a pound of sausage/liver.

19 Buy two litres of red wine and one litre of white wine.

20 Ask for five litres of beer.

21 Ask for a jar of coffee.

22 Ask for a bottle of mineral water.

23 Say you would like some fruit juice.

24 Ask for two cartons of milk.

25 Ask for a packet of tea.

26 Ask for a dozen eggs.

27 Find out where you can buy salt/pepper.

28 Ask for a slice of cheese.

Ich habe diesen Käse hier gekauft, aber er ist nicht gut.

29 Say you are buying food for a picnic.

30 Ask for two hundred grammes of butter.

31 Find out if they sell sweets/chocolate.

32 Ask for a packet of sugar.

33 Say you do not like it and that you are not going to buy it.

34 Say it is too dear.

35 Say he/she has given you too much/little.

36 Say you will take it.

37 Say you want nothing else.

38 Find out how much you owe.

39 Ask for change.

40 Say you bought this cheese here. Say it is not nice. Ask for your money back.

41 Say you only have a hundred-mark note.

42 Ask if you can choose the fruit.

43 Say a little bigger, please.

44 Ask if he/she has anything cheaper.

45 Find out where the cash desk is.

46 Ask for a box/plastic bag.

47 Find out if you can pay with a cheque or credit card.

48 Ask if they are open on Sunday.

49 Find out what time the shop opens.

50 Find out what time the shop shuts.

Wollen Sie auf Seite 73 verweisen.

Shopping for clothes and toiletries

MATERIALS

cotton	die Baumwolle (n.p.)
leather	das Leder (n.p.)
nylon	das Nylon (n.p.)
wool	die Wolle (n.p.)

SIZE OF CLOTHING

big	groß
long	lang
short	kurz
size	die Größe(n)
small	klein
tight	eng
too	zu
wide	breit/weit

BAD-WEATHER CLOTHES

anorak	der Anorak(s)
coat	der Mantel(¨)
glove	der Handschuh(e)
hat	der Hut(¨e)
pullover	der Pullover(-)
raincoat	der Regenmantel(¨)
scarf	der Schal(e)

GOOD-WEATHER CLOTHES

shorts	die Shorts (n.p.)
swimming-costume	der Badeanzug(¨e)/ die Badehose(n)
T-shirt	das T-shirt(s)

ON YOUR FEET

boot	der Stiefel(n)
shoe	der Schuh(e)
slipper	der Hausschuh(e)
sock	die Socke(n)

OTHER CLOTHES

blouse	die Bluse(n)
dress	das Kleid(er)
dressing-gown	der Morgenrock(¨e)
jacket	die Jacke(n)
jeans	die Jeans(-)
pyjamas	der Schlafanzug(¨e)
shirt	das Hemd(en)
skirt	der Rock (¨e)
suit	der Anzug(¨e)
tie	die Krawatte(n)
tights	die Strumpfhose(n)
trousers	die Hose(n)

TOILETRIES

comb	der Kamm(¨e)
shampoo	das Schampoo/das Haarwaschmittel
soap	die Seife(n)
toothbrush	die Zahnbürste(n)
toothpaste	die Zahnpasta

OTHER WORDS		VERBS	
changing cubicle	**der Umkleide-raum("e)**	to put on	**anziehen**
		to try on	**anprobieren**
clothes	**die Kleider**	to window-shop	**einen Schaufenster-**
handkerchief	**das Taschen-tuch("er)**		**bummel machen**
pair	**das Paar(e)**		

Du bist dran

1 Ask what size it is.

2 Ask what size the shoes are.

3 Ask if the shirt is cotton/nylon.

4 Ask if the pullover is made of wool.

5 Say you would like to buy some slippers.

6 Find out if the gloves are made of leather.

7 Say that you like this jacket.

8 Find out where the changing rooms are.

9 Say you would like to try on this pair of trousers.

10 Find out if they have the same skirt in blue.

11 Say the dress is too long/short/tight/wide/big/small.

12 Ask the assistant to gift-wrap the scarf.

13 Find out on which floor the men's department is.

14 Ask for the cash desk.

15 Find out where the lift/exit is.

16 Find out what time they open/close.

17 Ask if you can listen to this record.

18 Request a plastic bag.

19 Ask if you can exchange the coat.

20 Say that it is not your size.

21 Find out if there is another shop where you can buy a pullover.

22 Tell him/her that he/she has made a mistake.

23 Ask your friend which he/she is going to buy.

24 Ask if this T-shirt suits you.

25 Find out where you can buy soap/shampoo/a comb/a toothbrush/toothpaste.

26 Say you would like to window-shop.

27 Say that is too expensive.

28 Say it is very cheap.

29 Ask for your size.

30 Find out if they have anything cheaper.

31 Find out where you should pay.

Wollen Sie auf Seite 75 verweisen.

At the cleaner's/ launderette

GRUNDWORTSCHATZ

change (for washing-machine)	**das Kleingeld**	to clean	**reinigen**
		to mend (clothes)	**reparieren/ ausbessern**
cleaner's	**die Reinigung(en)**	washing-machine	**die Wasch-**
coin	**die Münze(n)**		**maschine(n)**
launderette	**der Waschsalon**	washing-powder	**das Waschpulver**

Du bist dran

1 Say you would like to have your trousers cleaned.

2 Ask if your blouse can be mended.

3 Find out when it will be ready.

4 Say you would like to wash these clothes.

5 Ask for change for the washing-machine.

6 Find out which coins are needed for the washing-machine.

7 Ask where you can buy washing-powder.

Wollen Sie auf Seite 77 verweisen.

At the café/restaurant

GRUNDWORTSCHATZ

ON THE TABLE

cup	die Tasse(n)
fork	die Gabel(n)
glass	das Glas(¨er)
knife	das Messer(-)
mustard	der Senf
pepper	der Pfeffer
plate	der Teller(-)
salt	das Salz
saucer	die Untertasse(n)
spoon	der Löffel(-)
tablecloth	die Tischdecke(n)/ das Tischtuch(¨er)
vinegar	der Essig

FACILITIES

area outside a café	die Terasse(n)
in the shade	im Schatten
in the sun	in der Sonne
telephone	das Telefon(e)
toilets	die Toiletten

ORDERING

dessert	der Nachtisch(e)/ das Dessert(s)
first course	der erste Gang
menu	die Speisekarte(n)
starter	die Vorspeise
waiter	der Kellner(-)
waitress	die Kellnerin(nen)

FOOD

breakfast	das Frühstück
chips	die Pommes Frites
cucumber	die Gurke(n)
ice-cream (vanilla, strawberry, chocolate)	das Vanilleeis/ Erdbeereis/ Schokoladeneis
mussels	die Muscheln
oysters	die Austern
pork chop	das Schweinekotelett
rice	der Reis
salad	der Salat
sandwich (cheese, ham sausage)	das Käsebrot/ Schinkenbrot/ Wurstbrot(e)
sardine	die Sardine(n)
soup	die Suppe(n)
trout	die Forelle(n)

See also pages 24-5 in the 'Shopping for food' section.

PAYING THE BILL

bill	die Rechnung(en)
included	inbegriffen/ einschließlich
owner	der Inhaber
mistake	der Fehler(-)
service	die Bedienung
tip	das Trinkgeld

OTHER WORDS		VERBS	
Cheers!	**Prost!**	to be hungry	**Hunger haben/ hungrig sein**
choice	**die Wahl**		
delicious	**ausgezeichnet/ lecker**	to be thirsty	**Durst haben/ durstig sein**
Enjoy your meal!	**Guten Appetit!**	to book	**reservieren**
ill	**krank**	to choose	**wählen**
feeling ill	**sich nicht wohl fühlen/jemanden nicht gut gehen**	to clean	**putzen**
		to feel ill	**sich nicht wohl fühlen/nicht gut gehen**
tray	**das Tablett(s)**		
		to order	**bestellen**

Du bist dran

1 Call the waiter/waitress and ask for the menu.

2 Say you would like to give a tip.

3 Say you would like to reserve a table.

4 Say you have reserved a table.

5 Ask the waiter for a cup/saucer/knife/fork/spoon/glass.

6 Say that the tablecloth is dirty.

7 Tell the waiter that you would like to order (now).

8 Ask the waiter to remove his tray.

9 Ask for the bill.

10 Say cheers and enjoy your meal.

11 Ask the waiter to choose/recommend a wine.

12 Find out where the telephone is/the toilets are.

13 Find out if service is included.

14 Say that you are hungry/thirsty.

15 Ask for two portions of wiener schnitzel.

16 Say that the meal is delicious.

17 Ask what he/she would like for dessert.

18 Say that you feel ill.

19 Ask for the wine list.

20 Ask the waiter to recommend something for today.

21 Ask for pork chop with onions, peas and chips.

22 Find out if breakfast is available.

23 Say you would like a black/a white coffee.

24 Order soup, chicken, rice/potatoes.

25 Say you would like a cheese/sausage/ham sandwich.

26 Order oysters/mussels.

Um wieviel Uhr wird das Frühstück serviert?

27 Order trout/sardines.

28 Say you would like some cucumber in the salad.

29 Ask for cherries/a banana/a melon/an orange/a peach/a pear/an apple/strawberries/apricots/pineapple/grapes.

30 Order chicken, beans, mushrooms and carrots.

31 Say you do not like cabbage.

32 Tell the waiter that the cauliflower is not nice.

33 Find out if you can have lamb today.

34 Find out what drinks they have.

35 Ask for a litre of white/red wine.

36 Order a half-litre of beer.

37 Say you would like some fruit juice/mineral water/milk/tea.

38 Say you would like a boiled/fried/poached/scrambled egg.

39 Ask for salt/pepper/vinegar/mustard.

40 Ask for a slice of ham.

41 Ask the waiter to clear the table.

42 Say you would like to be outside in the sun/shade.

43 Ask for a table for two near the window.

44 Tell the waiter that he has made a mistake.

45 Say you do not understand the menu. Ask what this dish is.

46 Ask him/her to close/open the window.

47 Ask for more.

48 Ask for an ashtray.

49 Tell the waiter he has forgotten the vanilla ice-cream.

50 Ask for change for the telephone.

51 Say the food is cold.

52 Say that your fork is dirty.

53 Say that you want something cold/hot to drink.

54 Say that you are too hot/cold.

55 Say that you only had a lemonade and an orange juice.

56 Ask him to check the bill.

57 Say you are in a hurry. Find out how long you must wait.

58 Say that there are four of you.

59 Explain to your friend that the dish is fish, not meat.

60 Find out if they accept credit cards.

61 Say you did not order any wine.

62 Find out if there is a choice of vegetables.

63 Say that it smells good.

64 Ask your friend if he/she has decided.

65 Say that it is too expensive.

66 Find out which wine he/she would like.

Wollen Sie auf Seite 77 verweisen.

At the post office ρ-80

GRUNDWORTSCHATZ

ITEMS TO SEND

letter	**der Brief(e)**
packet	**das Päckchen(-)**
parcel	**das Paket(e)**
postal order	**die Postan-weisung(en)**
postcard	**die Postkarte(n)**
postcard (picture)	**die Ansichtskarte(n)**
telegram	**das Telegramm(e)**

FACILITIES

counter	**der Schalter(-)**
phone booth	**die Telefonzelle(n)**
post-box	**der Briefkasten(¨)**
poste restante	**postlagernd**

SENDING THINGS OFF

abroad	**im Ausland**

address	**die Adresse(n)**
by airmail	**mit Luftpost**
80-pfennig stamp	**die Briefmarke zu 80 Pfennig**
Great Britain	**Großbritannien**

OTHER WORDS

coin	**die Münze(n)**
collection (of mail)	**die Sammlung(en)**
fragile	**zerbrechlich**
mail	**die Post**

VERBS

to fill in a form	**ein Formular ausfüllen**
to post	**aufgeben/einwerfen**
to send	**schicken**

Du bist dran

1 Ask where the post office is.

2 Ask if there is a post-box in the post office.

3 Find out how much it costs to send a letter/postcard to England.

4 Say you would like to send a letter to Great Britain.

5 Say you would like to send a parcel.

6 Find out if a packet has arrived for you.

7 Say you would like two 80-pfennig stamps.

8 Find out when the post office closes.

9 Ask if there is a poste restante letter for you.

10 Find out if there is a phone booth there.

11 Say you need coins for a phone call to England.

12 Say that you want to send a telegram.

13 Ask how much it is to send a telegram.

14 Find out how long it takes for a letter to reach Great Britain.

15 Ask if there is a special post-box for letters going abroad.

16 Find out where you can post a letter.

17 Say you would like to phone someone in England.

18 Say you would like to buy a postal order.

Sie wollen DM50,000? Sie müssen dieses Formular ausfüllen.

19 Find out which counter you need.

20 Say you want to send the letter by airmail.

21 Find out if you have fill in a form.

22 Ask if the post office is open on Saturday.

23 Find out if there is a faster service.

24 Ask when the next collection is.

25 Ask at what time the post office opens.

Wollen Sie auf Seite 80 verweisen.

On the telephone P. 81

GRUNDWORTSCHATZ

dialling tone	**das Amtszeichen**	phone call (trunk)	**das Ferngespräch(e)**
directory	**das Telefon-buch(¨er)**	phone number	**die Telefon-nummer(n)**
hello	**Hallo!**	reverse-charge call	**das R-Gespräch(e)**
operator	**die Vermittlung**		
phone call (local)	**das Ortsgespräch(e)**	to dial	**wählen**

Du bist dran

1 Find out where the nearest telephone is.

2 Ask for the telephone directory.

3 Ask if you can speak to Hans.

4 Say you can't hear the dialling tone.

5 Ask for the number of the tourist office.

6 Say you would like to speak to the operator.

7 Say you want to make a reverse-charge call.

8 When you have picked up the phone, say hello and say it is Melanie speaking.

9 Ask the caller if he/she wants to leave a message.

10 Say unfortunately you cannot hear well. Ask the caller to speak more slowly.

11 Ask the person not to hang up.

12 Say you have got the wrong number.

Wollen Sie auf Seite 81 verweisen.

Vermittlung? Ich möchte bitte Mars anrufen.

At the bank/ exchange office

P-82

GRUNDWORTSCHATZ

MONEY

currency	**die Währung**
pound sterling	**das englische Pfund**
ten-mark note	**der Zehnmark-schein(e)**

ITEMS TO TAKE

cheque card	**die Scheckkarte(n)**
credit card	**die Kreditkarte(n)**
passport	**der Reisepaß(¨sse)**
traveller's cheque	**der Reisescheck(s)**

OTHER WORDS

cashier's desk	**die Kasse(n)**

commission	**die Provision(en)**
counter	**der Schalter(-)**
per cent	**Prozent**
rate of exchange	**der Wechselkurs**

VERBS

to be worth	**wert sein**
to change	**wechseln**
to go to the cash desk	**an die) Kasse gehen zu der)**
to queue	**Schlange stehen/ sich anstellen**
to sign	**unterschreiben**

Du bist dran

1 Find out where you must queue.

2 Say you want to change some pounds into marks.

3 Say you want to change some traveller's cheques into marks.

4 Find out which counter you need.

5 Ask if it is your turn.

6 Ask what the rate of exchange is.

7 Ask if he/she wants to see your passport.

8 Say you have forgotten your passport.

9 Say you will fetch your passport.

10 Find out where you have to sign.

11 Find out how many Deutschmarks you will get for a pound.

12 Ask if you must go to the cashier's desk.

13 Say you have a credit card.

14 Say you have a banker's card.

15 Find out if you have to pay a commission.

16 Ask if the commission is ten per cent.

17 Say you would like 50-mark notes.

18 Say you would like some 5-mark coins.

19 Tell the clerk that all your money has been stolen.

20 Ask him/her to phone your bank in England.

21 Tell him/her to ask your bank to send some money.

Wollen Sie auf Seite 82 verweisen.

At the police station/ lost property office *P-83*

GRUNDWORTSCHATZ

PROPERTY		form (to fill in)	**das Formular(e)**
camera	**der Photoapparat (e)**	gold	**das Gold**
cheque-book	**das Scheckbuch(¨er)**	lost property office	**das Fundbüro(s)**
handbag	**die Handtasche(n)**		
passport	**der Reisepaß(¨sse)**	make (e.g. of camera)	**die Marke(n)**
purse	**das Portemonnaie(s)**		
ring	**der Ring(e)**	police station	**die Polizeiwache(n)**
suitcase	**der Koffer(-)**	reward	**die Belohnung(en)**
wallet	**die Brieftasche(n)**		
watch	**die Armbanduhr(en)**	**VERBS**	
		to borrow	**entleihen/borgen**
VILLAINS		to burgle	**einbrechen** (sep)
burglar	**der Einbrecher(-)**	to contain (in)	**sein/beinhalten**
thief	**der Dieb(e)**	to describe	**beschreiben**
		to leave (behind)	**liegenlassen** (sep)
OTHER WORDS		to lend	**leihen**
colour	**die Farbe(n)**	to lose	**verlieren**
description	**die Beschreib-ung(en)**	to run away	**weglaufen** (sep)
		to steal	**stehlen**

Du bist dran

1 Say that you have lost something. Find out where the police station is.

2 Say that you have found something. Find out where the lost property office is.

3 Say the camera is quite large.

4 Say that you do not know the make.

5 Say that you bought it two years ago.

6 Say that it is five years old.

7 Tell the policeman that it is worth £100.

8 Say that the suitcase contained clothes, a watch and a gold ring.

9 Say that the purse contained twenty pounds.

10 Say that the wallet contained five hundred marks.

11 Say that you did not see the thief/burglar.

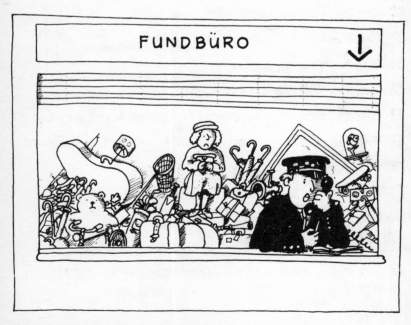

Sie haben Ihre Frau verloren? Ja, sie ist hier.

12 Say that you lost it in front of the ticket-office.

13 Say that you left it in your room.

14 Say that the suitcase was in your father's car.

15 Say that you lost it two hours ago/yesterday/the day before yesterday.

16 Ask if the ring has been found.

17 Say that you are a British tourist.

18 Say that the handbag is your sister's.

19 Say that the camera is yours.

20 Ask if you must pay.

21 Ask what you must do now.

22 Say that you will return tomorrow.

23 Say that you will write.

24 Say that you will phone.

25 Say that your car has been stolen.

26 Say that a lot of things have been stolen from your car.

27 Say that you have lost your traveller's cheques/passport.

28 Ask if you can borrow some money.

29 Ask if he/she can lend you some money.

30 Say that the thief ran away.

31 Say it was a present from your aunt.

32 Say that you are very angry/disappointed/surprised/ pleased.

Wollen Sie auf Seite 83 verweisen.

At the tourist information office

p. 84

GRUNDWORTSCHATZ

PLACES TO GO

amusement	**das Freizeit-angebot(e)**
circus	**der Zirkus**
concert	**das Konzert(e)**
disco	**die Diskothek(en)**
museum	**das Museum(een)**
place of interest	**die Sehenswürdig-keit(en)**
show	**die Aufführung(en)**
theatre	**das Theater(-)**
trip	**der Ausflug(¨e)**
zoo	**der Zoo/der Tier-garten(¨)**

INFORMATION

brochure	**(die Broschüre(n))/der Prospekte(e)**
information	**die Auskunft(¨e)**
map of the area	**die Regionalkarte/die Karte der Gegend**

timetable	**der Fahrplan(¨e)**
town plan	**der Stadtplan(¨e)**

OTHER WORDS

information office	**das Verkehr-samt(¨er)/die Auskunftsstelle(n)**
seat	**der Platz(¨e)**
ticket	**die Karte(n)**
tourist office	**das Verkehrs-amt(¨er)/Frem-denvenkehrs-amt(¨er)**

VERBS

to be interested in	**sich interessieren für** (+acc)
to book	**reservieren**
to go for walks	**spazieren-gehen** (sep)
to hire	**mieten**
to visit	**besuchen**

Du bist dran

1 Say you are a British tourist.

2 Ask if he/she can give you information on the area.

3 Find out if he/she has any brochures.

4 Ask for a map of the town.

5 Ask for a map of the area.

6 Ask for a bus timetable.

7 Ask for the address of a hotel/a campsite.

8 Find out what the places of interest are.

9 Ask for information about the castle.

10 Say you would like information about the museum.

11 Find out if there are any trips.

12 Ask what there is to do in the evenings.

13 Find out if there are any shows/amusements.

14 Find out what time the museum opens/closes.

15 Say you like sports. Find out if there are any facilities.

16 Ask if you can hire skis/a bicycle.

Sie wollen den Schloß heute abend besuchen? Sehr gut, Fräulein.

17 Ask if you can buy tickets here.

18 Find out if there is a circus/theatre/concert in the area.

19 Say you are interested in castles.

Wollen Sie auf Seite 84 verweisen.

Asking the way p.85

GRUNDWORTSCHATZ

DIRECTIONS

straight on	**immer geradeaus**
to (on) the left	**links**
to (on) the right	**rechts**

HOW TO GET THERE

by bus	**mit dem Bus**
by taxi	**mit dem Taxi**
by train	**mit dem Zug**
by tube	**mit der U-Bahn**
on foot	**zu Fuß**

LANDMARKS

bridge	**die Brücke(n)**
bus stop	**die Haltestelle(n)**
corner	**die Ecke(n)**
crossroads	**die Straßen-kreuzung(en)**
town centre	**die Stadtmitte(n)**
traffic-lights	**die Ampel(n)**
traffic island	**die Verkehrsinsel(n)**

POSITION

after	**nach**
at the end	**am Ende**
before	**vor**
behind	**hinter**
beside	**neben**
five kilometres away	**fünf Kilometer von hier**
five minutes away	**fünf Minuten von hier**
opposite	**gegenüber**

OTHER WORDS

area	**das Gebiet(e)**
first	**der/die/das erste**
map (of town)	**der Stadtplan(¨e)**
motorway	**die Autobahn(en)**
road-map	**die Straßenkarte(n)**
second	**der/die/das zweite**

VERBS

to carry on	**weiterfahren** (sep)
to cross	**überqueren**
to follow	**folgen** (+dat)
to get lost	**sich verirren**
to go down	**hinuntergehen** (sep)
to go up	**hinaufgehen** (sep)
to turn	**abbiegen** (sep)

Du bist dran

1 Say 'Excuse me' to a passer-by.

2 Say that you are lost.

3 Ask for directions to the town centre.

4 Ask if it is far.

5 Ask how far it is.

6 Tell him/her to turn right at the crossroads.

7 Tell him/her to turn left after the bank.

8 Tell him/her to cross the bridge and go straight on.

9 Tell him/her to go up the road to the supermarket.

10 Tell him/her to go down the road as far as the traffic-lights.

11 Say it is opposite the cinema.

12 Tell him/her to follow the road as far as the roundabout.

13 Say the bus stop is on the left.

14 Tell him/her to take the first road on the right.

15 Tell him/her to take the second road after the bus stop.

16 Tell him/her to go straight on as far as the corner of the street.

17 Find out if he/she has a road-map/map of the town.

18 Tell him/her to take the motorway.

19 Say that you do not know the area.

20 Tell him/her that it is five kilometres away.

21 Say it is five minutes' walk away.

22 Tell him/her to take a taxi/tube/bus.

23 Tell him/her that it is behind the baker's.

24 Find out what number bus you must take.

25 Say that you will go with him/her.

26 Tell him/her to go down the corridor and take the lift to the first floor.

27 Say you do not understand.

28 Ask him/her to repeat that.

29 Ask where you can find a taxi.

Wollen Sie auf Seite 85 verweisen.

Sie wollen nach Mars fahren? Fahren Sie bis zum Mond, dann fahren Sie nach rechts und dann fahren Sie zwei Jahre weiter und — da steht Mars.

At the cinema

P. 86

GRUNDWORTSCHATZ

TYPES OF FILM

adventure film	**der Abenteuerfilm(e)**
comedy film	**die Komödie(n)**
detective film	**der Kriminalfilm(e)**
horror film	**der Gruselfilm(e)**
romantic film	**der Liebesfilm(e)**
science-fiction film	**der Science-Fiction-Film(e)**
spy film	**der Agentenfilm(e)**
war film	**der Kriegsfilm(e)**
western	**der Western**

DETAILS OF FILM

English version	**in Englischer Sprache**

performance	**die Vorstellung(en)**
star	**der Star(s)**
subtitle	**der Untertitel(-)**

GETTING TO YOUR SEAT

seat	**der Platz("e)**
tip	**das Trinkgeld**
usherette	**die Platzanweiserin(nen)**

OTHER WORDS

circle	**der Balkon**
interval	**die Pause(n)**
stalls	**das Parkett**
to book	**reservieren**

Du bist dran

1 Ask your friend what film is showing at the cinema.

2 Find out if the film has English subtitles.

3 Find out if the film is in German.

4 Say you would like to book two seats.

5 Ask your friend if he/she would like to go to the cinema this evening.

6 Find out what time the film starts.

7 Find out what time the film finishes.

8 Find out if there is an interval.

9 Ask how much a seat in the circle costs.

10 Say you would like a seat in the stalls.

11 Say that you liked the film.

12 Say that you did not like the film.

13 Find out if there is a reduction for groups.

14 Say that you prefer detective films.

15 Suggest that you meet in front of the cinema.

16 Ask what sort of film it is.

17 When your friend says it was a bad film, say that you do not agree.

18 Ask your friend if he/she liked the film.

19 When your friend says the film was good, say you agree.

Wollen Sie auf Seite 86 verweisen.

At the hotel

P·87

GRUNDWORTSCHATZ

TYPES OF ROOM

double room	das Doppel-zimmer(-)
family room	das Mehrbettzimmer für Familien
room with two single beds	das Zimmer mit zwei (Einzel)betten
single room	das Einzelzimmer(-)

PLACES

bathroom	das Badezimmer(-)
car-park	der Parkplatz(¨e)
corridor	der Gang(¨e)
floor (i.e. storey)	der Stock(¨e)/ Stockwerk(e)
ground floor	im Erdgeschoß
lift	der Aufzug(¨e)
shower	die Dusche(n)
toilet	die Toilette

CHECKING IN AND OUT

bed	das Bett(en)
bill	die Rechnung(en)
cheque	der Scheck(s)
credit card	die Kreditkarte(n)
free (i.e. not occupied)	frei
full	voll
full board and lodging	Vollpension
half board	Halbpension

included	inbegriffen
luggage	das Gepäck (n.p.)
not included	nicht inbegriffen
number	die Nummer(n)
suitcase	der Koffer(-)

ITEMS YOU MIGHT NEED

blanket	die Decke (n)
coat-hanger	der Kleiderbügel(-)
key	der Schlüssel(-)
pillow	das Kopfkissen(-)
soap	die Seife(n)
toilet-paper	das Toilettenpapier
towel	das Handtuch(¨er)

COMPLAINTS

blocked	verstopft
leaky	undicht/tropfend
noise	der Lärm
tap	der Wasserhahn (Wasserhähne)
too much	zu viel

VERBS

to book	reservieren
to fill in a form	ein Formular ausfüllen
to park	parken
to work (i.e. to function	funktionieren

Du bist dran

1 Say you would like to reserve a room.

2 Say that you have reserved a room.

3 Say that you would like a single room.

4 Say that you would like a double room.

5 Say that you would like a room with a single bed.

6 Say that you would like a room with a double bed.

7 Say that you would like a room with twin beds.

8 Say that you would like a family room.

9 Ask if they have a room with a shower or a bathroom.

10 Say that you will stay for four nights.

11 Say that you would like to leave tomorrow morning.

12 Tell the receptionist that you would like to leave early.

13 Say that you want a room on the ground floor.

14 Ask what floor your room is on.

15 Find out the number of your room.

16 Find out if you can eat at the hotel.

17 Ask what time breakfast is.

18 Ask if breakfast is included.

19 Ask if they have a room free.

20 Say you are English/Irish/Scottish/Welsh.

21 Find out if you have to fill in a form.

22 Ask for your key.

23 Ask for your bill.

24 Say the bill is not correct.

25 Tell the receptionist that you would like to pay by cheque or credit card.

26 Find out if there is a cinema nearby.

27 Ask for directions to the dining-room.

28 Say that there is no soap in your room.

29 Say that you would like an extra pillow.

30 Say that you are not happy with your room. Ask them to phone another hotel.

31 Say you would like to complain.

32 Say that there is no towel in your room.

33 Say that you have lost your key.

34 Find out if they have anything cheaper.

35 Ask if you can take up your luggage now.

36 Find out if there is a car-park nearby.

37 Say you want a room which looks onto the beach.

38 Say you will take these rooms.

39 Tell the receptionist that you have reserved a room by telephone.

40 Tell the receptionist that the lift doesn't work.

41 Say you would like more coat-hangers.

42 Say that the tap is leaky.

43 Say that the light is not working.

44 Say that the wash-basin is blocked.

45 Say that your room is too noisy.

46 Tell the receptionist that you want a different room.

47 Say that you are very disappointed.

48 Ask the receptionist for another blanket.

Wollen Sie auf Seite 87 verweisen.

P.90

7

Visiting and receiving an exchange partner

SITING AND RECEIVING AN EXCHANGE PARTNER

GRUNDWORTSCHATZ

ON ARRIVAL

clothes	die Kleider
present (i.e. gift)	das Geschenk(e)
suitcase	der Koffer(-)
tired	müde
tiring	ermüdend
Welcome!	Willkommen!

IN THE BATHROOM

bath	das Bad("er)
shower	die Dusche(n)
soap	die Seife(n)
toothpaste	die Zahnpasta
towel	das Handtuch("er)

DESCRIBING YOURSELF OVER THE PHONE

curly (hair)	lockig
fat	dick
glasses	die Brille(n)
long (hair)	lang
quite	ziemlich
short (hair)	kurz
small	klein
straight (hair)	glatt

| tall | groß |
| thin | dünn |

OTHER WORDS

downstairs	unten
party (young people's)	die Party
upstairs	oben

VERBS

to borrow	entleihen/borgen
to clear the table	den Tisch abräumen
to do the washing-up	abspülen (sep)
to get to know	kennenlernen (sep)
to go to bed	ins Bett gehen
to help	helfen (+dat)
to hurt oneself	sich verletzen/sich weh tun
to introduce	vorstellen (sep)
to lay the table	den Tisch decken
to rest	sich ausruhen (sep)
to share	teilen
to show	zeigen

Du bist dran

1 Say that you are pleased to meet him/her.

2 Say that he/she is welcome.

3 Introduce him/her to your brother.

4 Say that it is a present from your parents.

5 Say that you have a brother and two sisters.

6 Find out where your room/the bathroom is.

7 Say you will show him/her to his/her room.

8 Tell him/her that the bathroom is upstairs, on the left.

9 Say that you would like to phone your parents.

10 Ask if he/she would like to phone his/her parents.

11 Find out what time breakfast is.

12 Tell your partner that breakfast is at eight o'clock.

13 Say you are tired and that you would like to go to bed.

14 Ask if he/she is tired.

15 Find out if he/she wants to go to bed.

16 Say that the journey was very tiring.

17 Say that you like German food.

18 Ask if he/she likes English food.

19 Say that you do not like cabbage.

20 Ask what he/she does not like.

21 Find out what time you leave tomorrow.

22 Ask where you can put your clothes.

23 Ask where you can put your suitcase.

24 Ask where you can meet.

25 Say you would like to meet his/her friends.

26 Ask if he/she would like to meet your friends.

27 Ask if there is anything in particular that he/she would like to do.

28 Find out what he/she wants to do.

29 Say you would like to go out.

30 Say that you would like to go to the beach.

31 Suggest that you meet in front of the station.

32 You are phoning your exchange partner. Say that you are tall/small.

33 Say that you wear glasses.

Ich möchte ein Zimmer nicht teilen.

34 Say that your hair is short/long.

35 Say that your hair is curly/straight.

36 Say that your hair is brown/black/fair.

37 Say that you will be wearing a green coat and jeans.

38 Say that you feel ill.

39 Say that you have hurt yourself.

40 Ask what he/she will be wearing.

41 Ask if he/she is ill.

42 Find out if he/she has hurt himself/herself.

43 Find out where you can wash your dirty clothes.

44 Ask if he/she has any dirty clothes.

45 Ask if you can watch the television.

46 Ask him/her if he/she wants to watch the television.

47 Say you would like to help his/her mother.

48 Say you will lay/clear the table.

49 Offer to wash the dishes.

50 Say that you would like to go to the party.

51 Ask if he/she wants to go to the party.

52 Find out how you will get back from the town.

53 Say that you can come back by bus.

54 Say that you do not want to share a room.

55 Ask if he/she has soap/a towel/toothpaste.

56 Say that you need soap/a towel/toothpaste.

57 Ask if he/she would like a bath/a shower.

58 Say that you would like to have a bath/shower.

59 Say you would like to rest.

60 Say you would like to borrow some money.

61 Say that you are hungry/thirsty.

62 Say that you are hot/cold.

Wollen Sie auf Seite 90 verweisen.

Die Antworten

Public transport

1 Einmal einfach nach Bonn, zweiter Klasse bitte.

2 Einmal hin und zurück nach Düsseldorf, erster Klasse bitte.

3 Zwei Fahrkarten bitte.

4 Gibt es einen Bus/einen Zug nach München?

5 Wann kommt er an?

6 Wann fährt er ab?

7 Wie oft fahren die Züge nach Bonn?

8 Ich möchte einen Platz reservieren.

9 Ich habe einen Platz reserviert.

10 Wo ist der Bahnhof/der Busbahnhof/die U-Bahnstation?

11 Wie lange dauert die Reise?

12 Wann ist der nächste Flug?

13 Wo ist der Fahrkartenschalter?

14 Wo ist das (Fremden)verkehrsbüro/das Auskunftsbüro/die Auskunftsstelle?

15 Wo ist die Gepäckaufbewahrung/das Fundbüro?

16 Von welchem Gleis fährt der Zug nach Bonn?

17 Wo ist der Taxistand/die Bushaltestelle?

18 Ist noch Platz frei in diesem Abteil?

19 Der Platz ist besetzt.

20 Wann startet/landet das Flugzeug?

21 Ich möchte ein Taxi nehmen.

22 Wo kann ich ein Taxi finden?

23 Fährt der Zug direkt?

24 Muß ich umsteigen?

25 Wo muß ich umsteigen?

26 Können Sie mich zu einem billigen Hotel fahren?

27 Wo ist die Imbißstube?

28 Wann fährt der nächste/erste/letzte Bus ab?

29 Ich möchte ein Nichtraucherabteil.

30 Wo kann ich mein Gepäck lassen?

31 Ist dies der richtige Bahnsteig?

32 Wo soll ich aussteigen?

33 Gibt es einen Speisewagen/einen Schlafwagen?

34 Gibt es eine Ermäßigung/einen Zuschlag?

35 Wo sind die Toiletten, bitte?

36 Wo ist der Wartesaal?

37 Darf ich hier mein Gepäck aufgeben?

38 Ist der Flug verspätet?

39 Ist der Zug früher angekommen?

40 Ich habe meine Fahrkarte verloren.

41 Was kostet ein Fahrkartenblock?

42 Haben Sie einen U-Bahnplan?

43 Ich werde um 22 Uhr ankommen.

44 Um 2 Uhr werde ich mich auf den Weg machen.

45 Hast du etwas zu verzollen?

46 Ich bin gerade angekommen.

47 Ich werde den Bus um 22 Uhr nehmen.

48 Ich habe versucht, vom Bahnhof anzurufen.

49 Ich werde vom Flughafen anrufen.

50 Wo kann ich einen Gepäckträger finden.

51 Können Sie mir mit meinem Gepäck helfen?

52 Ich habe meinen Bus versäumt (verpaßt).

53 Fährt dieser Bus zur Stadtmitte?

At the garage/filling station

1 Zwanzig Liter Super bitte.

2 Zehn Liter Bleifrei bitte.

3 Volltanken bitte.

4 Können Sie das Öl nachsehen?

5 Können Sie den Reifendruck überprüfen?

6 Können Sie das Wasser nachsehen?

7 Wo sind die Toiletten?

8 Verkaufen Sie Straßenkarten?

9 Geht es hier nach Bonn?

10 Wie komme ich am besten nach Düsseldorf?

11 Ist die Straße nach Bonn eine Bundesstraße oder eine Autobahn?

12 Wo kann ich parken?

13 Ich habe eine Autopanne.

14 Mein Wagen (Er) steht etwa zwei Kilometer von hier.

15 Können Sir mir helfen?

16 Können Sie mein Auto reparieren?

17 Ist ein Mechaniker frei?

18 Die Bremsen sind nicht in Ordnung.

19 Ich habe eine Reifenpanne.

20 Der Scheinwerfer ist nicht in Ordnung.

21 Die Windschutzscheibe ist kaputt.

22 Ich brauche eine neue Batterie.

23 Wieviel muß ich bezahlen?/Was bin ich schuldig?

24 Darf ich von hier telefonieren?

25 Wie weit ist Bonn von hier?

26 Wo ist das nächste Hotel?

27 Verkaufen Sie Süßigkeiten?

28 Können Sie bitte die Windschutzscheibe putzen?

29 Mir ist das Benzin ausgegangen.

30 Ich habe einen Unfall gehabt.

31 Wie lange muß ich warten?

32 Wieviel kostet es?

At the customs

1 Ich bin Engländer/Ire/Schotte/Waliser (Engländerin/Irin/Schottin/ Waliserin).

2 Ich habe nichts zu verzollen.

3 Ich möchte einen Photoapparat verzollen.

4 Ich habe zwei Koffer und eine Tasche.

5 Dieser Koffer gehört mir.

6 Es sind Kleider und Geschenke in meinem Koffer.

7 Ich habe die Armbanduhr vor einer Woche in der Schweiz gekauft.

8 Das Parfüm hat vierhundert Mark gekostet.

9 Wollen Sie meinen Reisepaß sehen?

10 Ich werde zwei Wochen in Deutschland bleiben.

11 Ich bin hier im Urlaub.

At the campsite

1 Ich möchte einen Platz reservieren.

2 Darf ich hier zelten?

3 Haben Sie Platz für ein Zelt?

4 Ich habe ein Zelt/einen Wohnwagen.

5 Was kostet es für ein Zelt, zwei Erwachsene, vier Kinder und ein Auto?

6 Ich möchte zwei Tage bleiben.

7 Ich bin alleine.

8 Ich werde übermorgen ankommen.

9 Ich werde am Samstag abfahren.

10 Wo ist mein Platz bitte?

11 Ich möchte einen Platz im Schatten.

12 Ich bin Engländer/Ire/Schotte/Waliser (Engländerin/Irin/Schottin/ Waliserin).

13 Wollen Sie meinen Ausweis/meinen Reisepaß sehen?

14 Wann muß ich bezahlen?

15 Ich möchte jetzt bezahlen.

16 Wie komme ich (am besten) zum Campingplatz?

17 Kann man hier warm duschen?

18 Ich möchte einen Platz in der Nähe von den Toiletten.

19 Wo kann man Trinkwasser bekommen?

20 Wo kann man Kleider waschen/abspülen?

21 Was sind die Regeln?

22 Mein Platz ist zu nahe bei den Mülltonnen.

23 Darf ich einen Dosenöffner/einen Korkenzieher/Streichhölzer entleihen?

24 Darf ich mein Zelt dort aufschlagen?

25 Wo ist die nächste Steckdose?

26 Was kostet es pro Person?

27 Es ist zu teuer.

28 Gibt es hier eine Waschmaschine?

29 Gibt es hier heißes Essen?

30 Gibt es hier einen Laden?

31 Darf ich ein Feuer machen?

32 Ich bin mit dem Campingplatz sehr zufrieden.

33 Hat der Campingplatz viele Einrichtungen?

34 Ich brauche Campinggas.

35 Ich brauche Batterien.

36 Ist der Campingplatz nachts gut beleuchtet?

37 Ist der Campingplatz nachts geschlossen?

38 Muß ich dafür einen Zuschlag bezahlen?

At the youth hostel

1 Ich habe ein Bett reserviert.

2 Ich habe kein Bett reserviert.

3 Gibt es noch Platz?

4 Sind noch Betten frei?

5 Ich werde morgen/übermorgen abfahren.

6 Ich werde drei Nächte bleiben.

7 Wir sind zwei Jungen und zwei Mädchen.

8 Ich bin Engländer/Ire/Schotte/Waliser (Engländerin/Irin/Schottin/ Waliserin).

9 Was kostet es pro Person pro Nacht?

10 Gibt es Läden in der Nähe?

11 Gibt es Duschen, eine Küche und einen Spielraum in der Jugendherberge?

12 Wo sind die Toiletten/die Abfalltonnen?

13 Ich möchte jetzt/später/morgen bezahlen.

14 Wann gibt es Frühstück/Mittagessen/Abendessen?

15 Um wieviel Uhr macht die Jugendherberge zu?

16 Wann hat das Büro morgens auf?

17 Was ist die Hausordnung?

18 Ich habe einen Schlafsack.

19 Ich möchte einen Schlafsack/einige Laken/einige Bettdecken mieten.

20 Wo sind die Mädchenschlafräume und die Jungenschlafräume?

21 Ist Alkohol erlaubt?

22 Um wieviel Uhr muß ich abfahren?

23 Muß ich ein Formular ausfüllen?

24 Gibt es warmes Wasser?

25 Was muß ich tun, bevor ich abfahre?

26 Wo kann ich meine Wertsachen lassen?

27 Ich möchte mich beschweren.

28 Wollen Sie meinen Ausweis sehen?

29 Ist die Jugendherberge voll?

30 Ist die Jugendherberge das ganze Jahr hindurch offen?

31 Darf ich in der Jugendherberge kochen?

32 Gibt es hier etwas zu essen?

33 Wie komme ich zum Speisesaal?

34 Wo kann ich mein Rad lassen?

35 Es tut mir leid. Ich möchte nicht oben schlafen. Haben Sie ein Bett im Erdgeschoß?

At the doctor's/at the scene of an accident

1 Können Sie mir helfen?

2 Können Sie bitte einen Arzt anrufen?

3 Können Sie einen Krankenwagen rufen?

4 Ich brauche einen Zahnarzt.

5 Ich möchte den Arzt aufsuchen.

6 Ich habe einen Unfall gehabt.

7 Ich habe Zahnweh.

8 Ich habe Halsschmerzen.

9 Ich habe Kopfschmerzen.

10 Ich habe Magenschmerzen.

11 Ich habe mir den Arm/das Bein gebrochen.

12 Er hat sich den Arm/das Bein gebrochen.

13 Ich bin erkältet.

14 Ich habe mich verbrannt.

15 Ich habe mir den Arm verbrannt.

16 Er hat einen Sonnenbrand/Sonnenstich.

17 Sie hat Grippe.

18 Ich habe mich geschnitten.

19 Ich habe mich am Bein/Finger (ins Bein/in den Finger) geschnitten.

20 Ich bin hingefallen.

21 Ich habe einen Autounfall gehabt.

22 Ich habe Fieber.

23 Ich bin seekrank.

24 Ein Insekt hat mich gestochen.

25 Ich habe einen Husten.

26 Ich habe mich dreimal übergeben.

27 Mein Freund (Meine Freundin) ist verletzt.

28 Soll ich den Arzt nochmal aufsuchen?

29 Soll ich im Bett bleiben?

30 Brauche ich ein Rezept?

31 Wo ist die Apotheke?

32 Ich möchte eine Quittung bitte.

33 Bis wann muß ich die Tabletten nehmen?

34 Ich möchte Watte, einen Verband, einige Pflaster und etwas Antiseptikum kaufen.

35 Meine Schwester fühlt sich krank (elend).

36 Ich möchte Kopfschmerztabletten bitte.

37 Ich bin krank seit zwei Stunden/seit gestern.

38 Wie oft soll ich die Tabletten nehmen?

39 Ich fühle mich elend/besser.

40 Haben Sie ein Mittel gegen Halsschmerzen?

41 Ich nehme keine Arznei.

42 Ich habe eine Versicherung./Ich bin versichert.

43 Können Sie die Polizei/die Feuerwehr anrufen?

44 Der Unfall war ernst.

45 Ich bin nicht (daran) schuld; der andere Fahrer war (daran) schuld.

46 Verkaufen Sie Salbe gegen Sonnenbrand?

47 Mein Vater hat gebremst: aber es gab einen Zusammenstoß.

48 Der Motor hat gebrannt.

49 Der Führerschein meines Vaters ist im Hotel.

50 Ein Radfahrer (Eine Radfahrerin) hat einen alten Mann beim Überqueren der Straße überfahren.

51 Es tut mir weh.

Shopping for food and drink

1 Ich möchte ein Brot bitte.

2 Was kostet es?

3 Ich möchte einige Stücke Kuchen kaufen.

4 Fünfhundert Gramm Schinken bitte.

5 Ich möchte etwas Rindfleisch/Hammelfleisch/Hähnchen.

6 Zweihundertfünfzig Gramm Wurst bitte.

7 Gibt es in der Nähe ein offenes Lebensmittelgeschäft?

8 Ich möchte Zigaretten für meinen Vater kaufen.

9 Zweihundert Gramm Kirschen/Bananen/Apfelsinen/Pfirsiche/ Birnen/Äpfel/Erdbeeren/Aprikosen/Trauben bitte.

10 Ich möchte eine Ananas/eine Melone.

11 Wo kann ich Gemüse kaufen?

12 Ich möchte ein Pfund Bohnen/Zwiebeln/Erbsen/Kartoffeln/ Champignons/Kohl/Karotten/Blumenkohl.

13 Einen Kopfsalat bitte.

14 Gibt es eine Metzgerei/Fleischerei in der Nähe?

15 Ich möchte ein Kilo Hähnchen/Schweinefleisch/Steak.

16 Ist das Fleisch gut bei jenem Händler?

17 Wo kann ich Meeresfrüchte kaufen?

18 Ich möchte ein Pfund Wurst/Leber.

19 Zwei Liter Rotwein und einen Liter Weißwein bitte.

20 Fünf Liter Bier bitte.

21 Ein Glas Kaffee bitte.

22 Eine Flasche Mineralwasser bitte.

23 Ich möchte Obstsaft.

24 Zwei Tüten Milch bitte.

25 Ein Päckchen Tee bitte.

26 Ein Dutzend Eier bitte.

27 Wo kann ich Salz/Pfeffer kaufen?

28 Eine Scheibe Käse bitte.

29 Ich möchte etwas für ein Picknick kaufen.

30 Zweihundert Gramm Butter.

31 Verkaufen Sie Bonbons/Schokolade?

32 Ein Päckchen Zucker bitte.

33 Das gefällt mir nicht. Ich kaufe es nicht.

34 Das ist zu teuer.

35 Sie haben mir zu viel/zu wenig gegeben.

36 Das nehme ich.

37 Das ist alles, danke.

38 Was kostet das bitte?

39 Ich möchte Kleingeld bitte.

40 Ich habe diesen Käse hier gekauft aber er schmeckt nicht gut. Können Sie mir mein Geld zurückgeben?

41 Ich habe nur einen Hundertmarkschein.

42 Darf ich selbst das Obst wählen?

43 Etwas größer bitte.

44 Haben Sie etwas Billigeres?

45 Wo ist die Kasse?

46 Ich möchte einen Karton/eine Plastiktüte.

47 Darf ich mit Scheck oder Kreditkarte bezahlen?

48 Ist das Geschäft am Sonntag geöffnet?

49 Wann macht der Laden auf?

50 Wann schließt der Laden?

Shopping for clothes and toiletries

1 Welche Größe ist es?

2 Welche Größe hat der Schuh?

3 Ist das Hemd aus Baumwolle/aus Nylon?

4 Ist der Pullover aus Wolle?

5 Ich würde gern Hausschuhe kaufen.

6 Sind die Handschuhe aus Leder?

7 Diese Jacke gefällt mir.

8 Wo sind die Umkleideräume?

9 Ich möchte diese Hose anprobieren.

10 Haben Sie denselben Rock in Blau?

11 Das Kleid ist zu lang/kurz/eng/weit/klein.

12 Können Sie den Schal als Geschenk einpacken?

13 In welchem Stock ist die Herrenabteilung?

14 Wo ist die Kasse bitte?

15 Wo ist der Aufzug/der Ausgang bitte?

16 Wann macht dieses Kaufhaus auf/zu?

17 Darf ich diese Schallplatte anhören?

18 Ich möchte eine Plastiktüte.

19 Kann ich den Mantel umtauschen?

20 Das ist nicht meine Größe.

21 Gibt es einen anderen Laden, in dem ich einen Pullover kaufen kann?

22 Entschuldigen Sie, aber Sie haben einen Fehler gemacht.

23 Was willst du kaufen?

24 Paßt mir dieses T-Shirt gut?

25 Wo kann ich Seife/Haarshampoo/einen Kamm/eine Zahnbürste/Zahnpasta kaufen?

26 Ich möchte einen Schaufensterbummel machen.

27 Das ist zu teuer.

28 Es ist sehr billig.

29 Haben Sie meine Größe?

30 Haben Sie etwas Billigeres?

31 Wo soll ich bezahlen?

At the cleaner's/launderette

1 Ich möchte meine Hose reinigen lassen.

2 Können Sie meine Bluse ausbessern?

3 Wann ist es fertig?

4 Ich möchte diese Kleider waschen.

5 Haben Sie Kleingeld für die Waschmaschine?

6 Was für Münzen braucht man für die Waschmaschine?

7 Wo kann ich Waschpulver kaufen?

At the café/restaurant

1 Herr Ober!/Fräulein! Die Speisekarte bitte!

2 Ich möchte ein Trinkgeld geben.

3 Ich möchte einen Tisch reservieren.

4 Ich habe einen Tisch reserviert.

5 Herr Ober! Ich möchte eine Tasse/eine Untertasse/ein Messer/
eine Gabel/einen Löffel/ein Glas.

6 Die Tischdecke ist schmutzig.

7 Ich möchte (jetzt) bestellen.

8 Können Sie bitte Ihr Tablett wegnehmen?

9 Zahlen bitte!/Die Rechnung bitte!

10 Prosit! Guten Appetit!

11 Können Sie einen Wein wählen/empfehlen?

12 Wo ist das Telefon?/Wo sind die Toiletten?

13 Ist die Bedienung inbegriffen?

14 Ich bin hungrig/durstig. (Ich habe Hunger/Durst.)

15 Zweimal Wiener Schnitzel bitte.

16 Das Essen ist prima/ausgezeichnet/lecker!

17 Was wollen Sie als Nachtisch?

18 Ich bin krank. (Ich fühle mich nicht wohl/Es geht mir nicht gut.)

19 Die Weinkarte bitte.

20 Was können Sie heute empfehlen?

21 Ich möchte ein Schweinekotelett mit Zwiebeln, Erbsen und Pommes Frites.

22 Gibt es hier Frühstück?

23 Ich möchte einen Kaffee/einen Kaffee mit Milch.

24 Ich möchte Suppe, Hähnchen, Reis und Kartoffeln.

25 Ich möchte ein Käsebrot/Wurstbrot/Schinkenbrot.

26 Ich möchte Austern/Muscheln bitte.

27 Ich möchte eine Forelle/Sardinen.

28 Ich möchte eine Gurke in dem Salat.

29 Ich möchte Kirschen/eine Banane/eine Melone/eine Apfelsine/einen Pfirsich/eine Birne/einen Apfel/Erdbeeren/Aprikosen/Ananas/Trauben.

30 Ich möchte ein halbes Hähnchen, Bohnen, Champignons und Karotten.

31 Kohl schmeckt mir nicht.

32 Der Blumenkohl schmeckt nicht gut.

33 Gibt es heute Lammfleisch?

34 Was für Getränke haben Sie?

35 Einen Liter Rotwein/Weißwein bitte.

36 Eine Maß Bier bitte.

37 Ich möchte Obstsaft/Mineralwasser/Milch/Tee.

38 Ich möchte ein gekochtes Ei/ein Spiegelei/ein pochiertes (ein verlorenes) Ei/ein Rührei.

39 Ich möchte Salz/Pfeffer/Essig/Senf.

40 Ich möchte eine Scheibe Schinken.

41 Können Sie den Tisch abräumen?

42 Ich möchte draußen in der Sonne/im Schatten sitzen.

43 Bitte einen Tisch am Fenster für zwei Personen.

44 Entschuldigen Sie bitte. Sie haben einen Fehler gemacht.

45 Ich verstehe die Speisekarte nicht. Was ist das für ein Gericht?

46 Können Sie bitte das Fenster schließen/öffnen?

47 Noch mehr bitte!

48 Haben Sie einen Aschenbecher?

49 Sie haben das Vanilleeis vergessen.

50 Haben Sie Kleingeld für das Telefon?

51 Das Essen ist kalt.

52 Meine Gabel ist schmutzig.

53 Ich möchte etwas Kaltes/Heißes zu trinken.

54 Mir ist zu heiß/kalt.

55 Ich hatte nur eine Limonade und einen Orangensaft.

56 Können Sie die Rechnung nachprüfen?

57 Ich habe es eilig. Wie lange muß ich warten?

58 Wir sind zu viert.

59 Das ist kein Fleisch, sondern Fisch.

60 Nehmen Sie Kreditkarten?

61 Wein habe ich nicht bestellt.

62 Gibt es eine Auswahl an Gemüsen?

63 Das riecht (ja) gut!

64 Hast du dich entschieden?

65 Es ist zu teuer.

66 Welchen Wein möchtest du?

At the post office

1 Wo ist die Post/das Postamt?

2 Gibt es einen Briefkasten in der Post (im Postamt)?

3 Was kostet es, einen Brief/eine Postkarte nach England zu schicken?

4 Ich möchte einen Brief nach Großbritannien schicken.

5 Ich möchte ein Paket schicken.

6 Gibt es hier ein Paket für mich?

7 Ich möchte zwei Briefmarken zu achtzig Pfennig.

8 Wann macht die Post (das Postamt) zu? (Wann schließt die Post?)

9 Gibt es einen postlagernden Brief für mich?

10 Gibt es hier eine Fernsprechzelle?

11 Ich brauche Münzen für ein Ferngespräch nach England.

12 Ich möchte ein Telegramm schicken.

13 Was kostet es, ein Telegramm zu schicken?

14 Wie lange dauert es, bis ein Brief in Großbritannien ankommt?

15 Wo kann man Auslandsbriefe einstecken?

16 Wo kann ich einen Brief abgeben?

17 Ich möchte jemanden in England anrufen.

18 Ich möchte eine Postanweisung kaufen.

19 Welchen Schalter brauche ich?

20 Ich möchte diesen Brief per Luftpost schicken.

21 Muß ich ein Formular ausfüllen?

22 Ist die Post (das Postamt) am Samstag geöffnet?

23 Gibt es einen schnelleren Postdienst?

24 Wann ist die nächste Sammlung?

25 Um wieviel Uhr macht die Post (das Postamt) auf?

On the telephone

1 Entschuldigen Sie bitte. Wo ist das nächste Telefon?

2 Haben Sie das Telefonbuch bitte?

3 Kann ich Hans sprechen?

4 Ich kann das Amtszeichen nicht hören.

5 Wie ist die Nummer des Verkehrsamts bitte?

6 Kann ich die Vermittlung sprechen?

7 Ich möchte ein R-Gespräch anmelden.

8 Hallo. Hier spricht Melanie.

9 Wollen Sie etwas ausrichten lassen?

10 Ich kann Sie leider nicht gut verstehen. Sprechen Sie bitte langsamer.

11 Bitte legen Sie nicht auf.

12 Sie sind falsch verbunden.

At the bank/exchange office

1 Wo muß ich Schlange stehen? (Wo muß ich mich anstellen?)

2 Ich möchte einige Pfund in D-Mark wechseln.

3 Ich möchte einige Reiseschecks in D-Mark einlösen.

4 Welchen Schalter brauche ich?

5 Bin ich an der Reihe?

6 Welchen Wechselkurs haben Sie heute?

7 Wollen Sie meinen Paß sehen?

8 Ich habe meinen Paß vergessen.

9 Ich werde meinen Paß holen.

10 Wo muß ich unterschreiben?

11 Wieviele Deutschmark bekomme ich für ein Pfund?

12 Muß ich zur Kasse gehen?

13 Ich habe eine Kreditkarte.

14 Ich habe eine Scheckkarte.

15 Muß ich eine Provision bezahlen?

16 Ist die Provision zehn Prozent?

17 Ich möchte Fünfzigmarkscheine.

18 Ich möchte Fünfmarkstücke.

19 Mein Geld wurde gestohlen.

20 Können Sie meine Bank in England anrufen?

21 Können Sie meine Bank darum bitten, Geld zu senden.

At the police station/ lost-property office

1 Ich habe etwas verloren. Wo ist die nächste Polizeiwache?

2 Ich habe etwas gefunden. Wo ist das Fundbüro?

3 Der Photoapparat ist ziemlich groß.

4 Die Marke kenne ich nicht.

5 Ich habe ihn/sie/es vor zwei Jahren gekauft.

6 Er/Sie/Es ist fünf Jahre alt.

7 Er/Sie/Es ist hundert Pfund wert.

8 Der Koffer enthielt Kleider, eine Armbanduhr und einen Ring aus Gold.

9 Das Portemonnaie enthielt zwanzig Pfund.

10 Die Brieftasche enthielt fünfhundert Mark.

11 Ich haben den Dieb/den Einbrecher nicht gesehen.

12 Ich habe ihn/sie/es vor dem Schalter verloren.

13 Ich habe ihn/sie/es in meinem Zimmer liegengelassen.

14 Der Koffer war im Auto meines Vaters.

15 Ich habe ihn/sie/es vor zwei Stunden/gestern/vorgestern verloren.

16 Hat man meinen Ring gefunden?

17 Ich bin ein britischer Tourist/eine britische Touristin.

18 Die Handtasche gehört meiner Schwester.

19 Der Photoapparat gehört mir.

20 Muß ich bezahlen?

21 Was muß ich jetzt tun?

22 Ich werde morgen zurückkommen.

23 Ich werde schreiben.

24 Ich werde anrufen.

25 Mein Auto wurde gestohlen.

26 Viele Sachen wurden von meinem Auto gestohlen.

27 Ich habe meine Reiseschecks/meinen Paß verloren.

28 Darf ich etwas Geld entleihen?

29 Können Sie mir etwas Geld leihen?

30 Der Dieb ist weggelaufen.

31 Er/Sie/Es war ein Geschenk von meiner Tante.

32 Ich bin sehr böse/enttäuscht/erstaunt/froh.

At the tourist information office

1 Ich bin ein britischer Tourist/eine britische Touristin.

2 Können Sie mir Auskunft über die Gegend geben?

3 Haben Sie Prospekte?

4 Haben Sie einen Stadtplan bitte?

5 Haben Sie eine Landkarte von der Gegend?

6 Haben Sie einen Busfahrplan bitte?

7 Geben Sie mir die Adresse eines Hotels/eines Campingplatzes.

8 Was sind die Sehenswürdigkeiten?

9 Haben Sie Auskunft über das Schloß?

10 Ich möchte Auskunft über das Museum, bitte.

11 Gibt es Ausflüge?

12 Was gibt es am Abend (abends) zu tun? (Was kann man abends machen?)

13 Gibt es Aufführungen/Unterhaltungsmöglichkeiten?

14 Wann macht das Museum auf/zu?

15 Ich habe Sport gern. Gibt es Sportmöglichkeiten?

16 Kann ich Skier/ein Rad mieten?

17 Kann ich hier Karten kaufen?

18 Gibt es einen Zirkus/ein Theater/ein Konzert in der Gegend?

19 Ich interessiere mich für Schlösser.

Asking the way

1 Entschuldigen Sie, bitte.

2 Ich habe mich verirrt.

3 Wie komme ich (am besten) zur Stadtmitte?

4 Ist das weit von hier?

5 Wie weit ist das von hier?

6 Biegen Sie an der nächsten Kreuzung rechts ab.

7 Biegen Sie nach der Bank links ab.

8 Gehen Sie über die Brücke und dann immer geradeaus.

9 Gehen Sie die Straße hinauf, bis zum Supermarkt.

10 Gehen Sie die Straße hinab, bis zur Verkehrsampel.

11 Er/Sie/Es steht dem Kino gegenüber.

12 Folgen Sie der Straße bis zum Kreisverkehr.

13 Die Bushaltestelle ist an der linken Seite (links).

14 Nehmen Sie die erste Straße rechts (an der rechten Seite).

15 Nehmen Sie die zweite Straße hinter der Bushaltestelle.

16 Gehen Sie immer geradeaus bis zur Straßenecke.

17 Haben Sie eine Straßenkarte/einen Stadtplan?

18 Nehmen Sie die Autobahn.

19 (Ich bin hier fremd) Ich kenne diese Gegend nicht.

20 Er/Sie/Es ist fünf Kilometer entfernt (von hier).

21 Er/Sie/Es ist fünf Minuten zu Fuß entfernt (von hier).

22 Nehmen Sie ein Taxi/eine U-Bahn/einen Bus.

23 Er/Sie/Es ist hinter der Bäckerei.

24 Welche Buslinie soll ich nehmen?

25 Ich gehe (fahre) mit Ihnen.

26 Gehen Sie den Gang hinab, und nehmen Sie den Aufzug bis zum ersten Stock.

27 Ich verstehe nicht.

28 Können Sie das bitte wiederholen?

29 Wo bekomme ich ein Taxi?

At the cinema

1 Welcher Film läuft im Moment im Kino?

2 Hat der Film englische Untertitel?

3 Ist der Film auf Deutsch?

4 Ich möchte zwei Plätze reservieren.

5 Möchtest du heute Abend ins Kino gehen?

6 Wann beginnt der Film?

7 Wann ist der Film zu Ende?

8 Gibt es eine Pause?

9 Was kostet ein Platz im Balkon?

10 Ich möchte einen Platz im Parkett.

11 Der Film hat mir gut gefallen.

12 Der Film hat mir nicht gefallen.

13 Gibt es eine Gruppenermäßigung?

14 Ich habe lieber Kriminalfilme (Krimis).

15 Wir können uns vor dem Kino treffen.

16 Was für ein Film ist das?

17 Nein, das stimmt nicht!

18 Hat der Film dir gefallen?

19 Ja, das stimmt!

At the hotel

1 Ich möchte ein Zimmer reservieren.

2 Ich habe ein Zimmer reserviert.

3 Ich möchte ein Einzelzimmer.

4 Ich möchte ein Doppelzimmer.

5 Ich möchte ein Zimmer mit einem Einzelbett.

6 Ich möchte ein Zimmer mit einem Doppelbett.

7 Ich möchte ein Zimmer mit zwei Einzelbetten.

8 Ich möchte ein Familienzimmer/ein Mehrbettzimmer für Familien.

9 Haben Sie ein Zimmer mit Dusche oder Bad?

10 Ich werde vier Nächte bleiben.

11 Ich möchte morgen Abend abfahren.

12 Ich möchte früh abfahren.

13 Ich möchte ein Zimmer im Erdgeschoß.

14 In welchem Stock ist mein Zimmer?

15 Was ist die Nummer meines Zimmers?

16 Kann man hier im Hotel essen?

17 Wann (Um wieviel Uhr) ist das Frühstück?

18 Ist das Frühstück inbegriffen?

19 Haben Sie ein Zimmer frei?

20 Ich bin Engländer/Ire/Schotte/Waliser (Engländerin/Irin/Schottin/Waliserin).

21 Muß ich ein Formular ausfüllen?

22 Ich möchte meinen Schlüssel bitte.

23 Ich möchte meine Rechnung bitte.

24 Es stimmt etwas nicht mit der Rechnung. (Die Rechnung stimmt nicht.)

25 Ich möchte mit Scheck oder mit Kreditkarte bezahlen.

26 Gibt es ein Kino in der Nähe?

27 Wie komme ich zum Eßzimmer/Speisezimmer?

28 Es gibt keine Seife in meinem Zimmer.

29 Ich möchte noch ein Kopfkissen.

30 Ich bin mit dem Zimmer nicht zufrieden. Können Sie bitte ein anderes Hotel anrufen?

31 Ich möchte mich beschweren.

32 Es gibt kein Handtuch in meinem Zimmer.

33 Ich habe meinen Schlüssel verloren.

34 Haben Sie etwas Billigeres?

35 Darf ich jetzt mein Gepäck hinauftragen?

36 Gibt es einen Parkplatz in der Nähe?

37 Ich möchte ein Zimmer mit Blick auf den Strand.

38 Ich nehme diese Zimmer.

39 Ich habe ein Zimmer per Telefon reserviert.

40 Der Aufzug funktioniert nicht (ist außer Betrieb).

41 Ich möchte noch mehr Kleiderbügel bitte.

42 Der Wasserhahn ist undicht.

43 Die Lampe funktioniert nicht.

44 Das Waschbecken ist verstopft.

45 Mein Zimmer ist zu laut.

46 Ich möchte ein anderes Zimmer.

47 Ich bin sehr enttäuscht.

48 Haben Sie noch eine (Bett)decke bitte?

Visiting and receiving an exchange partner

1 Es freut mich dich kennenzulernen.

2 Du bist hier willkommen.

3 Darf ich dir meinen Bruder vorstellen?

4 Es ist ein Geschenk von meinen Eltern.

5 Ich habe einen Bruder und zwei Schwestern.

6 Wo ist mein Zimmer/das Badezimmer?

7 Ich zeige dir dein Zimmer.

8 Das Badezimmer ist oben links (auf der linken Seite).

9 Ich möchte meine Eltern anrufen.

10 Möchtest du deine Eltern anrufen?

11 Um wieviel Uhr ist das Frühstück?

12 Das Frühstück ist um acht Uhr.

13 Ich bin müde und ich möchte ins Bett gehen.

14 Bist du müde?

15 Möchtest du ins Bett gehen?

16 Die Reise war sehr ermüdend.

17 Das deutsche Essen schmeckt mir.

18 Schmeckt dir das englische Essen?

19 Ich mag Kohl nicht.

20 Was ißt du nicht gern?

21 Wann fährt man morgen ab?

22 Wohin kann ich meine Kleider hängen?

23 Wo kann ich meinen Koffer lassen?

24 Wo können wir uns treffen?

25 Ich möchte deine Freunde kennenlernen.

26 Möchtest du meine Freunde kennenlernen.

27 Möchtest du etwas besonders gern tun?

28 Was möchtest du tun?

29 Ich möchte gerne ausgehen.

30 Ich möchte gerne zum Strand gehen.

31 Wir können uns vor dem Bahnhof treffen.

32 Ich bin groß/klein.

33 Ich trage eine Brille.

34 Ich habe kurzes/langes Haar.

35 Ich habe lockiges/glattes Haar.

36 Mein Haar ist braun/schwarz/blond.

37 Ich werde einen grünen Mantel und Jeans tragen.

38 Es geht mir nicht sehr gut./Ich bin krank.

39 Ich habe mich verletzt.

40 Was wirst du tragen?

41 Bist du krank?

42 Hast du dich verletzt?

43 Wo kann ich meine verschmutzten Kleider waschen?

44 Hast du verschmutzte Kleider?

45 Darf ich fernsehen?

46 Möchtest du fernsehen?

47 Ich möchte deiner Mutter helfen.

48 Ich werde den Tisch decken/abräumen.

49 Darf ich abspülen?

50 Ich möchte gerne zu einer Party gehen.

51 Möchtest du zu einer Party gehen?

52 Wie kommt man von der Stadt/nach Hause zurück.

53 Man kann mit dem Bus zurückkommen.

54 Ich möchte ein Zimmer für mich alleine.

55 Hast du Seife/ein Badetuch/Zahnpasta?

56 Ich brauche Seife/ein Badetuch/Zahnpasta.

57 Möchtest du baden/duschen?

58 Ich möchte gerne baden/duschen.

59 Ich möchte mich gerne ausruhen.

60 Ich möchte gerne etwas Geld entleihen/borgen.

61 Ich bin hungrig/durstig. (Ich habe Hunger/Durst.)

62 Mir ist heiß/kalt.